Principles of Prayer

Principles of Prayer

Charles G. Finney

Compiled & Edited by
Louis Gifford Parkhurst, Jr.

 Bethany Fellowship INC.
MINNEAPOLIS, MINNESOTA 55438

Copyright © 1980
Louis Gifford Parkhurst, Jr.
All rights reserved

Published by Bethany Fellowship, Inc.
6820 Auto Club Road, Minneapolis, Minnesota 55438

Printed in the United States of America

Library of Congress Cataloging in Publication Data

Finney, Charles Grandison, 1792-1875.
    Principles of prayer.

    Bibliography: p.
    1. Prayer—Meditations.   I. Parkhurst, Louis
Gifford, 1946-   II. Title.
BV213.F56   1980   248.3'2   80-17856
ISBN 0-87123-468-8

To

Patricia Ann, Jonathan Edward
and Kathryn Elizabeth

who enrich my life with
every word and action

CHARLES G. FINNEY
"Young Man of Prayer"

Sketch by Todd Key

CHARLES G. FINNEY was America's foremost evangelist. Over half a million people were converted under his ministry in an age that offered neither amplifiers nor mass communication as tools. Harvard Professor, Perry Miller, affirmed that "Finney led America out of the eighteenth century." As a theologian, he is best known for his "Revival Lectures" and his "Systematic Theology."

LOUIS GIFFORD PARKHURST, JR., is pastor of First Christian Church of Rochester, Minnesota. He garnered a B.A. and an M.A. from the University of Oklahoma and an M.Div. degree from Princeton Theological Seminary. Before his ordination he was a graduate assistant at the University of Oklahoma. He is married and the father of two young children.

CONTENTS

INTRODUCTION

Why should every Christian become a master of Charles G. Finney's principles of prayer? Because every Christian wants principles that are true to the clear teaching of Scripture, that are sound and reasonable, and that have been verified by experience. Millions have been blessed by these principles; countless multitudes brought to the Savior; and great work for His Kingdom accomplished. In his memoirs Finney wrote that during his revival efforts he spoke to Christians and, "endeavored to make them understand that God would immediately answer prayer, provided they fulfilled the conditions upon which He had promised to answer prayer; and especially if they believed, in the sense of expecting Him to answer their requests."* When a Christian brings faith in the Lord to the conditions outlined in this book, God will answer every prayer. Finney's principles of prayer were themselves born from much labored prayer, and the appendix to this book illustrates some of the great effects of prayer in America and England.

I have edited this book because I believe Finney's time-honored principles will transform the lives of individuals who are searching for a trustworthy guide to Christian prayer. These principles, likewise, will transform any church when practiced by one or more members. Charles Finney mastered God's Word, and he applied the principles of effective prayer to every endeavor. God's Word and prayer will unlock the door to valuable service in the Kingdom of God for every Christian today just as they did for Finney and the Christians who supported his work. Finney bowed beneath the authority of Scripture because he found

---

*Charles G. Finney, an Autobiography, pp. 170, 171.

Scripture to be reasonable, life changing, and true—the very Word of God. Consequently, Finney applied the Scriptures as divine truth to the whole of his life including his study of prayer. He allowed God to master him and to speak to him in prayer. Through his devout and holy life, Finney became one of the most effective co-workers with God in the nineteenth century. His influence is felt today through the straightforward and explicitly Christian principles of prayer which he has left us.

For many years Finney's principles of prayer have lain buried in his massive tome *Lectures on Revivals of Religion*. Only a few in this century have dared to immerse themselves in and master this book entirely. Others have quickly passed through its pages for historical interest, and many have missed the truly educational value of Finney's thoughts on prayer. When Finney made a few modifications on his lectures in his more mature years, published as *Reflections on Revival*, he did not change his thoughts about prayer. Indeed, he said he should have emphasized more the influence of the Holy Spirit in the conversion of sinners; in other words, he wished he had emphasized more the necessity of fulfilling the conditions of prayer and of engaging in much prayer. Where he made some helpful expansions on prayer in his *Reflections on Revival*, they have been included in this volume. Finney applied his principles faithfully, consistently, and successfully throughout the course of his life and ministry. Now for the first time they are readily available in an accessible format for those who seek to spread the love and glory of God's Kingdom as they grow to Christian maturity.

Finney's principles have been condensed into 40 short meditations to aid in their study and mastery. The book can be read quickly in one or two sittings, but more value will be gained from daily meditation and application for 40 days. Read the meditation, reflect upon it, seek application to your life, and pray over it and through it. I have written the short prayers that follow each devotional in an attempt to reflect briefly the truth that Finney imparted to me, and my sense of appreciation to God for using Finney's principles to lift me beyond my own ignorance and inadequacy before God. I believe the cumulative and gradual application of these principles of prayer will change your life, but I cannot emphasize too strongly that they will have no lasting effect unless you "take time daily" to study, think, and pray through each of these meditations during your quiet time with the Scriptures. As Jacob wrestled with the angel and prevailed, so must we wrestle with these principles and learn to prevail with God.

Finally, I would like to express my gratitude to Dave Birch, Jr. who, after completing a tour with Youth With A Mission, introduced me to the writings and theology of Charles G. Finney and significantly enriched my ministry with the truth. May his own ministry continue to be blessed by our Lord as he applies these principles of prayer.

I also owe thanks to Harry Conn for his friendship and his lectures that so effectively apply Finney's principles to the present. I wish to thank Mr. Clyde Nealy of Men for Missions for locating the books by Finney which I have listed in the bibliography. This book would never have been completed nor my writing career commenced if I had not received encouragement and support from my wife, Patricia Ann, an ever-faithful partner in the ministry. For advice in technical areas I wish to thank my friend Jack Key, author, and librarian of the Mayo Clinic. For an example in prayer I wish to thank my father and mother and my prayer partner friend, Nowell Herzog.

With Thanksgiving to God,

L. G. Parkhurst, Jr.
First Christian Church
Rochester, Minnesota
November 22, 1979

Prevailing Prayer

"Prevailing, or effectual prayer, is that prayer which attains the blessing that it seeks. It is that prayer which effectually moves God. The very idea of *effectual* prayer is that it affects its object."

1. THE TRUTH AND PRAYER

There are two kinds of means requisite to promote a revival: the one to influence men, the other to influence God. The truth is employed to influence men, and prayer to move God. When I speak of moving God, I do not mean that God's mind is changed by prayer, or that His disposition or character is changed. But prayer produces such a change *in us* as renders it consistent for God to do as it would not be consistent for Him to do otherwise. When a sinner repents, that state of feeling makes it proper for God to forgive him. God has always been ready to forgive him on that condition, so that when the sinner changes his feelings and repents, it requires no change of feeling in God to pardon him. It is the sinner's repentance that renders His forgiveness proper, and is the occasion of God's acting as he does. So when Christians offer effectual prayer, their state of feeling renders it proper for God to answer them. He was never unwilling to bestow the blessing—on the condition that they felt aright, and offered the right kind of prayer.

Truth, by itself, will never produce the effect, without the Spirit of God, and the Spirit is given in answer to prayer. Sometimes it happens that those who are the most engaged in employing truth are not the most engaged in prayer. This is always unhappy. For unless they have the spirit of prayer (or unless someone else has), the truth, by itself, will do nothing but harden men in impenitence. Probably in the Day of Judgment it will be found that nothing is ever done by the truth, used ever so zealously, unless there is a spirit of prayer somewhere in connection with the presentation of truth.

Others err in the reverse direction. Not that they lay too much stress on prayer. But they overlook the fact that prayer might be offered forever, by itself, and nothing would be done. Because sinners are not converted by direct contact of the Holy Ghost, but by the truth, employed as a means. To expect the conversion of sinners by prayer alone, without the employment of truth, is to tempt God.

Prayer

"O God, send your Holy Spirit into my life that I might be changed; that I might be conformed to your will. Convict me of the truth through the Good News of your Son. Empower me with a true love for sinners that I might desire to keep them in my prayers and share with any the truth. Amen."

2. PRAY FOR SOMETHING DEFINITE

Many people go away into their rooms alone "to pray," simply because "they must say their prayers." The time has come when they are in the habit of going by themselves for prayer—in the morning, or at noon, or at whatever time of day it may be. But instead of having anything to say, any definite object before their mind, they fall down on their knees and pray for just what comes into their minds—for everything that floats in the imagination at the time, and when they have done they can hardly tell a word of what they have been praying for. This is not effectual prayer. What should we think of anybody who should try to move a Legislature so, and should say: "Now it is winter, and the Legislature is in session, and it is time to send up petitions," and should go up to the Legislature and petition at random, without any definite object? Do you think such petitions would move the Legislature?

A man must have some definite object before his mind. He cannot pray effectually for a variety of objects at once. The mind is so constituted that it cannot fasten its desires intensely upon many things at the same time. All the instances of effectual prayer recorded in the Bible are of this kind. Wherever you see that the blessing sought for in prayer was attained, you will find that the prayer which was offered was prayer for that definite object.

Prayer

"Dear Heavenly Father, my mind wanders so in my

prayers to you. My attention span is short; and I am soon off on other pursuits. Fix in my mind those people, events, or things for which I am to pray. Help me to fix my mind steadily, without wavering, on one purpose only, that I might accomplish through prayer at least one thing for your glory. Amen."

3. PRAY FOR THE WILL OF GOD

To pray for things contrary to the revealed will of God is to tempt God. There are three ways in which God's will is revealed to men for their guidance in prayer.

1. By express promises or predictions in the Bible, that He will give or do certain things; promises in regard to particular things, or in general terms, so that we may apply them to particular things. For instance, there is this promise: "What things soever ye desire, when ye pray, believe that ye receive them, and ye shall have them" (Mark 11:24).

2. Sometimes God reveals His will by His Providence. When He makes it clear that such and such events are about to take place, it is as much a revelation as if He had written it in His Word. It would be impossible to reveal everything in the Bible. But God often makes it clear to those who have spiritual discernment that it is His will to grant such and such blessings.

3. By His Spirit. When God's people are at a loss what to pray for, agreeable to His will, His Spirit often instructs them. Where there is no particular revelation, and Providence leaves it dark, and we know not what to pray for as we ought, we are expressly told that "the Spirit also helpeth our infirmities," and "the Spirit itself maketh intercession for us with groanings which cannot be uttered" (Rom. 8:26). It is just as plain here as if it were now revealed by a voice from heaven, that the Spirit of God helps the people of God to pray according to the will of God when they themselves know not what they ought to pray for. "And he that searcheth the hearts knoweth what is the mind of the Spir-

it, because he maketh intercession for the saints according to the will of God" (Rom. 8:27); and He leads Christians to pray for just those things, "with groanings which cannot be uttered." When neither the Word nor Providence enables them to decide, let them be "filled with the Spirit," as God commands them to be. He says: "Be filled with the Spirit" (Eph. 5:18). And *He* will lead their minds to such things as God is willing to grant.

Prayer

"Dear God, I confess that quite often I do not know how to pray as I ought, and I compound my sin by blundering on ahead at full steam anyway. Help me to dig deeply into the Scriptures that I might apply what I learn to my prayers. Help me to be more sensitive to the divine dimension in life around me that I might pray according to your providential governance. Bless me with a greater awareness of your Spirit as He moves within me that I might pray for whatever you would desire of me. Amen."

4. PRAY SUBMITTING TO GOD'S WILL

To pray effectually you must pray with submission to the will of God. Do not confound submission with indifference. No two things are more unlike each other. I once knew an individual who came where there was a revival. He himself was cold, and did not enter into the spirit of it, and had no spirit of prayer; and when he heard the brethren pray as if they could not be denied, he was shocked at their boldness, and kept all the time insisting on the importance of praying with submission; when it was as plain as anything could be that he confounded submission with indifference.

Again, do not confound submission in prayer with a general confidence that God will do what is right. It is proper to have this confidence that God will do right in all things. But this is a different thing from submission. What I mean by submission in prayer is acquiescence in the revealed will of God. To submit to any *command* of God is to obey it. Submission to some supposable or possible, but secret, decree of God is not submission. To submit to any dispensation of Providence is impossible till it comes. For we never can know what the event is to be till it takes place.

While the will of God is not known, to submit, without prayer, is tempting God. Perhaps, and for aught you know, the fact of your offering the right kind of prayer may be the thing on which the event turns. In the case of an impenitent friend, the very condition on which he is to be saved from hell may be the fervency and importunity of your prayer for that individual.

Prayer

"Dear Father, I always end my prayers by submitting to your will; but now it appears that I sometimes do not pray earnestly for what I desire and the good that I would accomplish, but simply turn it all over for you to take care of while I try to be satisfied with the results. Help me to wrestle with the strength and will of Jacob in my prayers, and then submit to obeying whatever you ask of me. Amen."

5. PRAY WITH WORTHY DESIRE

Effectual prayer for an object implies a desire for that object commensurate with its importance. If a person *truly* desires any blessing, his desires will bear some proportion to the greatness of the blessing. The desires of the Lord Jesus Christ for the blessing He prayed for were amazingly strong, amounting even to agony. If the desire for an object is strong, and is a benevolent desire, and the thing is not contrary to the will and providence of God, the presumption is that it will be granted. There are two reasons for the presumption:

1. The general benevolence of God. If it is a desirable object; if, so far as we can see, it would be an act of benevolence in God to grant it, His general benevolence is presumptive evidence that He will grant it.

2. If you find yourself exercised with benevolent desires for any object, there is a strong presumption that the Spirit of God is exciting these very desires, and stirring you up to pray for that object, so that it may be granted in answer to prayer. In such a case no degree of desire or importunity in prayer is improper. A Christian may come up, as it were, and take hold of the hand of God. See the case of Jacob when he exclaimed, in an agony of desire: "I will not let thee go, except thou bless me" (Gen. 32:26). Was God displeased with his boldness and importunity? Not at all; instead He granted him the very thing he prayed for.

So in the case of Moses. God said to him: "Let me alone, that my wrath may wax hot against them, and that I may consume them; and I will make of thee a great nation" (Ex. 32:10). What did Moses do? Did he stand aside and let God do as He said? No; his mind runs back to the Egyptians and he thinks how they will triumph. "Wherefore should the Egyptians speak, and say, For mischief did he bring them out?" (Ex. 32:11). It seemed as if he took hold of the uplifted hand of God to avert the blow. Did God rebuke him and tell him he had no business to interfere? No; it seemed as if He was unable to deny anything to such importunity, and so Moses stood in the gap and prevailed with God.

Prayer

"O Lord, there is much about prayer that I do not understand. How can I pray and prevail? Do my needs and desires that seem so paltry really merit the pleading and agony which men like Jacob, Moses, and Jesus expressed in their prayers? Open my eyes beyond myself that I might see the great needs of your Church and your world, and enable me to pray for these needs with all my heart, mind, soul, and strength. Amen."

6. PRAY WITH RIGHT MOTIVES

Prayer, to be effectual, must be offered from right motives. Prayer should not be selfish, but should be dictated by a supreme regard for the glory of God. A great deal is offered from pure selfishness. Women sometimes pray for their husbands that they may be converted, because, they say, "it would be so much more pleasant to have my husband go to church with me," and all that. And they seem never to lift up their thoughts above self at all. They do not seem to think how their husbands are dishonoring God by their sins, nor how God would be glorified in their conversion.

So it is very often with parents. They cannot bear to think that *their* children should be lost. They pray for them very earnestly indeed. But if you talk with them upon the subject, they are very tender about it and tell you how good their children are—how they respect religion, and how they are, indeed, "almost Christians now"; and so they talk as if they were afraid you would hurt their children by simply telling them the truth. They do not think how such amiable and lovely children are dishonoring God by their sins; they are only thinking what a dreadful thing it will be for them to go to hell. Unless their thoughts rise higher than this, their prayers will never prevail with a holy God.

The temptation to selfish motives is so strong that there is reason to fear a great many parental prayers never rise above the yearnings of parental tenderness. And that is the reason why so many prayers are not answered and why so many pious, praying parents have ungodly children.

Much of the prayer for the heathen world seems to be

based on no higher principle than sympathy. Missionary agents and others are dwelling almost exclusively upon the six hundred millions of heathens going to hell, while little is said of their dishonoring God. This is a great evil, and until the Church learns to have higher motives for prayer and missionary effort than sympathy for the heathen, her prayers and efforts will never amount to much.

Prayer

"Dear Father, help me to examine myself and my prayers that I might determine if they are truly from right motives. I have never thought about the seriousness of some of my petitions. I have offered up my needs and the needs of others, and I have failed to see that many of these petitions, though seemingly good on the outside, were really rooted in selfishness. Create in me a clean heart, O God, and renew a right spirit within me. Amen."

7. PERSEVERE WITH THE HOLY SPIRIT

Prayer, to be effectual, must be by the intercession of the Spirit. You never can expect to offer prayer according to the will of God without the Spirit. There must be a faith such as is produced by the effectual operation of the Holy Ghost.

As a general thing, Christians who have backslidden and lost the spirit of prayer will not get at once into the *habit* of persevering prayer. Their minds are not in a right state, and they cannot fix their thoughts so as to hold on till the blessing comes. If their minds were in that state in which they would persevere till the answer came, effectual prayer might be offered at once, as well as after praying ever so many times for an object. But they have to pray again and again, because their thoughts are so apt to wander away and are so easily diverted from the object.

Most Christians come up to prevailing prayer by a protracted process. Their minds gradually become filled with anxiety about an object, so that they will even go about their business sighing out their desires to God. Just as the mother whose child is sick goes round her house sighing as if her heart would break. And if she is a praying mother, her sighs are breathed out to God all the day long. If she goes out of the room where her child is, her mind is still on it; and if she is asleep, still her thoughts are on it, and she starts in her dreams, thinking that perhaps the child may be dying. Her whole mind is absorbed in that sick child. This is the state of mind in which Christians offer prevailing prayer.

Now, do not deceive yourselves with thinking that you offer effectual prayer without this intense desire for the blessing. I do not believe in it. Prayer is not effectual unless it is offered up with an agony of desire. The Apostle Paul speaks of it as a travail of the soul. Jesus Christ, when He was praying in the garden, was in such an agony that "his sweat was as it were great drops of blood falling down to the ground" (Luke 22:44).

Prayer

"O Lord, when I compare my feeble attempts at prayer with the standards for effective prayer, I confess that I do not pray to you but simply play at prayer. Forgive me for taking the blessings that are wrought from prayer so lightly that I have not been willing to persevere as I should, but have so soon given up and have turned the matter too quickly to you. Fill me now with the Spirit and the desire for persevering prayer. Amen."

8. PRAY OFTEN, RENOUNCING SINS, IN CHRIST'S NAME

If you mean to pray effectually, you must pray a great deal. It was said of the Apostle James that after he was dead it was found that his knees were callous, like a camel's knees, by praying so much. Ah, here was the secret of the success of those primitive ministers! They had callous knees!

You cannot prevail in prayer without renouncing all your sins. You must not only recall them to mind, and repent of them, but you must actually renounce them, leave them off, and in the purpose of your heart renounce them all forever.

If you intend prayer to be effectual, you must offer it in the name of Christ. You cannot come to God in your own name. You cannot plead your own merits. But you can come in a name that is always acceptable. You all know what it is to *use the name* of a man. If you should go to the bank with a draft or note, endorsed by John Jacob Astor, that would be giving you his name, and you could get the money from the bank just as well as he could himself. Now, Jesus Christ gives you the use of His name. And when you pray in the name of Christ the meaning of it is, that you can prevail just as well as He himself could, and receive just as much as God's well-beloved Son would if He himself were to pray for the same things. But you must pray in faith.

Prayer

"Dear Heavenly Father, I confess that I take the easy way in prayer, doing most of it as I recline in the comfort of

my bed or sitting in the chair of my desk. I don't really humble myself before you or work at prayer as I do anything else of importance. Forgive me and help me to renounce my foolish ways that I might accomplish great things through prayer for the glory of your kingdom. I pray in the Name you honor, even Jesus Christ my Lord. Amen."

9. PRAY IN FAITH

You must pray in faith. You must expect to obtain the things for which you ask. Do not look for an answer to prayer if you pray without any expectation of obtaining it. You are not to form such expectations without any reason for them. In the cases I have supposed, there is a reason for the expectation. If the thing is revealed in God's Word, and you pray without an expectation of receiving the blessings, you just make God a liar. If the will of God is indicated by His providence, you ought to depend on it, according to the clearness of the indication, so far as to expect the blessing if you pray for it. And if you are led by His Spirit to pray for certain things, you have as much reason to expect those things to be done as if God had revealed it in His Word.

But some say: "Will not this view of the leadings of the Spirit of God lead people into fanaticism?" I answer that I know not but many may deceive themselves in respect to this matter. Multitudes have deceived themselves in regard to all the other points of religion. And if some people should think they are led by the Spirit of God, when it is nothing but their own imagination, is that any reason why those who know that they are led by the Spirit should not follow the Spirit? Many people suppose themselves to be converted when they are not. Is that any reason why we should not cleave to the Lord Jesus Christ? Suppose some people are deceived in thinking they love God, is that any reason why the pious saint who knows he has the love of God shed abroad in his heart should not give vent to his feelings in songs of praise?

Some may deceive themselves in thinking they are led

by the Spirit of God. But there is no need of being deceived. If people follow impulses, it is their own fault. I do not want you to follow impulses. I want you to be sober-minded and follow the sober, rational leadings of the Spirit of God. There are those who understand what I mean, and who know very well what it is to give themselves up to the Spirit of God in prayer.

Prayer

"Lord Jesus, I do believe, but help my unbelief. I long to feel the leading of the Holy Spirit in my life, and I long to pray in faith knowing my prayers will be answered. It is a new insight for me to know that the sober and rational and intelligent decisions of my life made prayerfully can be the leadings of the Spirit of God rather than emotional impulses. Help me not to take too much for granted, but to look to the truth that real faith brings to those who seek to serve God. Amen."

10. WHY GOD REQUIRES STRONG DESIRE

These strong desires vividly illustrate the strength of God's feelings. They are like the real feelings of God for impenitent sinners. When I have seen, as I sometimes have, the amazing strength of love for souls that has been felt by Christians, I have been wonderfully impressed with the amazing love of God and His desires for their salvation.

The case of a certain woman, of whom I read, in a revival, made the greatest impression on my mind. She had such an unutterable compassion and love for souls that she actually panted for breath. What must be the strength of the desire which God feels when His Spirit produces in Christians such amazing agony, such throes of soul, such *travail*—God has chosen the best word to express it: it is travail—travail of the soul.

The soul of a Christian, when it is thus burdened, must have relief. God rolls this weight upon the soul of a Christian for the purpose of bringing him nearer to himself. Christians are often so unbelieving that they will not exercise proper faith in God till He rolls this burden upon them so heavily that they cannot live under it, but must go to Him for relief. It is like the case of many a convicted sinner. God is willing to receive him at once if he will come right to Him with faith in Jesus Christ. But the sinner will not come. He hangs back, and struggles, and groans under the burden of his sins, and will not throw himself upon God till his burden of conviction becomes so great that he can live no longer; and when he is driven to desperation, as it were, and feels as if he were ready to sink into hell, he makes a mighty plunge and throws himself upon God's mercy as his only hope. It was his duty to come before. God had no delight in his distress for its own sake.

So, when professors of religion get loaded down with the weight of souls, they often pray again and again, and yet the burden is not gone, nor their distress abated, because they have never thrown it all upon God in faith. But they cannot get rid of the burden. So long as their benevolence continues, it will remain and increase; and unless they resist and quench the Holy Ghost, they can get no relief until at length, when they are driven to extremity, they make a desperate effort, roll the burden upon the Lord Jesus Christ, and exercise a childlike confidence in Him. Then they feel relieved; then they feel as if the soul they were praying for would be saved. The burden is gone, and God seems in kindness to soothe the mind with a sweet assurance that the blessing will be granted.

Often, after a Christian has had this struggle, this agony in prayer, and has obtained relief in this way, you will find the sweetest and most heavenly affections flow out—the soul rests sweetly and gloriously in God and rejoices "with joy unspeakable and full of glory."

Do you ask why we never have such things here? I tell you it is not at all because you are so much wiser than Christians are in rural districts, or because you have so much more intelligence or more enlarged views of the nature of religion, or a more stable and well-regulated piety. I tell you, no. Instead of priding yourselves in being free from such extravagances, you ought to hide your heads, because Christians in the city are so worldly, and have so much starch, pride, and fashion that they cannot *come down* to such spirituality as this.

Prayer

"O Lord, my God, I love my friends, and I love those within my church, my Bible class, and my prayer group, but I hardly love the sinner. I confess that I still have feelings of resentment and sometimes even hate for those who have personally wronged me or the church. Please teach me to love and have feelings for all people, especially those who have wronged you and dishonored your Name. I turn them over to you now in childlike faith that you will hear my prayer. Amen."

11. PRAYER BRINGS UNITY AND BLESSING

Doubtless one great reason why God requires the exercise of this agonizing prayer is that it forms such a bond of union between Christ and the Church. It creates such a sympathy between them. It is as if Christ comes and pours the overflowings of His own benevolent heart into His people, and leads them to sympathize and to cooperate with Him as they never do in any other way.

This travailing in birth for souls creates also a remarkable bond of union between warm-hearted Christians and the young converts. Those who are converted appear very dear to the hearts that have had this spirit of prayer for them. The feeling is like that of a mother for her firstborn. Paul expresses it beautifully when he says: "My little children!" His heart was warm and tender to them. "My little children, of whom I travail in birth *again*"—they had backslidden, and he has all the agonies of a parent over a wandering child—"I travail in birth again until Christ be formed in you" (Gal. 4:19).

In a revival I have often noticed how those who had the spirit of prayer loved the young converts. I know this is all so much algebra to those who have never felt it. But to those who have experienced the agony of wrestling, prevailing prayer, for the conversion of a soul, you may depend upon it, that the soul, after it is converted, appears as dear as a child. You have agonized for it, received it in answer to prayer, and can present it before the Lord Jesus Christ, saying: "Behold, I and the children whom the Lord hath given me" (Isa. 8:18. See also Heb. 2:13).

Another reason why God requires this sort of prayer is that it is the only way in which the Church can be properly prepared to receive great blessings without being injured by them. When the Church is thus prostrated in the dust before God, and is in the depth of agony in prayer, the blessing does them good. While at the same time, if they had received the blessing without this deep prostration of soul, it would have puffed them up with pride. But as it is, it increases their holiness, their love, their humility.

Prayer

"Dear Heavenly Father, unite me more firmly with your Son, Jesus Christ. Fill my heart with His benevolent love for all people. Give me a real concern for those who are lost around me; those who have no one to turn to, and help me to share the message of Christ's love for us all, with them. Keep me humble and ever aware that every accomplishment for you is your work in me and in the church I serve. Amen."

12. A FINAL REMARK

A great deal of prayer is lost, and many people never prevail in prayer, because when they have *desires* for particular blessings, they do not follow them up. They may have desires, benevolent and pure, which are excited by the Spirit of God; and when they have them, they should persevere in prayer, for if they turn off their attention, they will quench the Spirit. When you find these holy desires in your minds:

1. Do not quench the Spirit.
2. Do not be diverted to other objects.

Follow the leadings of the Spirit till you have offered that "effectual fervent prayer" that "availeth much" (James 5:16).

Without the spirit of prayer, ministers will do but little good. A minister need not expect much success unless he prays for it. *Sometimes* others may have the spirit of prayer and obtain a blessing on his labors. Generally, however, those preachers are the most successful who themselves have most of the spirit of prayer.

Not only must ministers have the spirit of prayer, but it is necessary that the church should unite in offering that effectual fervent prayer which can prevail with God. "I will yet for this be inquired of by the house of Israel, to do it" (Ezek. 36:37).

Prayer

"Dear God, you have shown me through the teachings of Jesus, His apostles, and the prophets that you desire to

hear and answer my prayers. You desire that my prayers prevail with you for the salvation of the lost, the growth in grace of the church, and the deepening of my own relationship with you. May I no longer take prayer for granted, but really dedicate myself today to practicing what I have learned from a master on prayer, and through practice experience the joy and glory of prevailing and travailing with you. Amen."

Sources for "Prevailing Prayer"

Definition: *Revivals of Religion*, p. 50.

 1. Ibid., pp. 49, 50.
 2. Ibid., p. 51.
 3. Ibid., pp. 51, 52.
 4. Ibid., p. 53.
 5. Ibid., p. 54.
 6. Ibid., pp. 55, 56.
 7. Ibid., pp. 56-58.
 8. Ibid., pp. 63, 64.
 9. Ibid., pp. 64, 65.
10. Ibid., pp. 65, 67, 68.
11. Ibid., pp. 70, 71.
12. Ibid., p. 73.

Prayer of Faith

"To prove that faith is indispensable to prevailing prayer, it is only necessary to repeat what the apostle James expressly tells us: 'If any of you lack wisdom, let him ask of God, that giveth to all men liberally, and upbraideth not; and it shall be given him. But let him ask in faith, nothing wavering. For he that wavereth is like a wave of the sea driven with the wind and tossed' (James 1:5, 6)."

1. WHAT TO BELIEVE WHEN YOU PRAY

We are to believe in the existence of God. "He that cometh to God must believe that he *is*"—and in His willingness to answer prayer—"that he is, and that he is a rewarder of them that diligently seek him" (Heb. 11:6). There are many who believe in the existence of God but do not believe in the efficacy of prayer. They profess to believe in God but deny the necessity or influence of prayer.

We are to believe that we shall receive—something—what? Not something, or anything, as it happens; but some particular thing we ask for. We are not to think that God is such a Being, that if we ask for a fish, He will give us a serpent; or if we ask for bread, He will give us a stone. But He says: "*What things soever ye desire*, when ye pray, believe that ye receive *them*, and ye shall have them" (Mark 11:24).

With respect to the faith of miracles, it is plain that the disciples were bound to believe they should receive just what they asked for—that the very thing itself should come to pass. That is what they were to believe. Now, what ought men to believe in regard to other blessings? Is it a mere loose idea that if a man prays for a specific blessing, God will by some mysterious sovereignty give something or other to him, or something to somebody else, somewhere? When a man prays for his children's conversion, is he to believe that either his children will be converted or somebody else's children—it is altogether uncertain which? No, this is utter nonsense, and highly dishonorable of God. We are to believe that we shall receive the *very things* that we ask for.

Prayer

"Dear Heavenly Father, these are deep and weighty thoughts for me. I have always prayed 'Thy will be done,' because I didn't dare believe that you would always give me whatever I asked. Help me to understand these truths fully that I might ask rightly, that I might always pray for the very things that you would have for me. Amen."

2. PRAY FOR GOD'S PROMISES

Faith must always have evidence. A man cannot believe a thing unless he sees something which he supposes to be evidence. He is under no obligation to believe, and has no right to believe, a thing will be done unless he has evidence. It is the height of fanaticism to believe without evidence. The kinds of evidence a man may have are the following:*

1. Where God has *especially promised* the thing. As, for instance, when God says He is more ready to give His Holy Spirit to them that *ask* Him than parents are to give bread to their children. Here we are bound to believe that we shall receive it when we pray for it. You have no right to put an *if*, and say, "Lord, *if it be Thy will*, give us Thy Holy Spirit." This is to insult God. To put an *if* into God's promise where God has put none is tantamount to charging God with being insincere. It is like saying: "O God, if Thou art in earnest in making these promises, grant us the blessing we pray for."

2. Where there is a *general promise* in the Scriptures which you may reasonably apply to the particular case before you. If its real meaning includes the particular thing for which you pray, or if you can reasonably apply the principle of the promise to the case, there you have evidence. For instance, suppose it is a time when wickedness prevails greatly, and you are led to pray for God's interference. What promise have you? Why, this one: "When the enemy shall come in like a flood, the Spirit of the Lord shall lift up a standard against him" (Isa. 59:19). Here you see a general

---

Kinds of evidence continued in sections 3 and 4.

promise, laying down a principle of God's administration, which you may apply to the case before you as a warrant for exercising faith in prayer. And if the inquiry is made as to the *time* in which God will grant blessings in answer to prayer, you have this promise: "While they are yet speaking, I will hear" (Isa. 65:24).

There are general promises and principles laid down in the Bible which Christians might make use of if they would only *think*. Whenever you are in circumstances to which the promises or principles apply, you are to use them.

I could go from one end of the Bible to the other and produce an astonishing variety of texts that are applicable as promises—enough to prove that in whatever circumstances a child of God may be placed, God has provided in the Bible some promise, either general or particular, which he can apply, that is precisely suited to his case. Many of God's promises are very broad, on purpose, to cover much ground. What can be broader than the promise in our text: "What things soever ye desire when ye pray"?

Prayer

"O Lord Jesus, shine the light of your Holy Spirit into my mind as I more diligently search the Holy Scriptures for the promises you have for me and the world about me. Call to my mind those things that I have read when I am in time of trouble and distress, that I might pray rightly through the application of your promise to my need. Amen."

3. PRAY FOR PROPHETIC DECLARATIONS

3. Where there is any *prophetic declaration* that the thing prayed for is agreeable to the will of God. When it is plain from prophecy that the event is certainly to come, you are bound to believe it and to make it the ground for your special faith in prayer. If the time is not specified in the Bible, and there is no evidence from other sources, you are not bound to believe that it shall take place now, or immediately. But if the time is specified, or if the time may be learned from the study of the prophecies, and it appears to have arrived, then Christians are under obligation to understand and apply it by offering the prayer of faith. For instance, take the case of Daniel in regard to the return of the Jews from captivity. What does he say? "I Daniel understood by books the number of the years, whereof the word of the Lord came to Jeremiah the prophet, that he would accomplish seventy years in the desolations of Jerusalem" (Dan. 9:2). Here he learned from books; that is, he studied his Bible, and in that way understood that the length of the captivity was to be seventy years.

What does he do then? Does he sit down upon the promise and say: "God has pledged himself to put an end to the captivity in seventy years, and the time has expired, and there is no need to do anything"? Oh, no. He says: "And I set my face unto the Lord God, to seek by prayer and supplications, with fasting, and sackcloth, and ashes" (v. 3). He set himself at once to pray that the thing might be accomplished. He prayed in faith. But what was he to believe? What he had learned from the prophecy.

There are many prophecies yet unfulfilled, in the Bible, which Christians are bound to understand, as far as they are capable of understanding them, and then make them the basis of believing prayer. Do not think, as some seem to do, that because a thing is foretold in prophecy it is not necessary to pray for it, or that it will come whether or not Christians pray for it. God says in regard to this very class of events which are revealed in prophecy: "I will yet for this be inquired of by the house of Israel, to do it for them" (Ezek. 36:37).

Prayer

"O Lord, guide my reading of the Scriptures that I might have greater discernment of the truth, that I might discern the words of prophecy that apply to my life and my time. Guide me in my prayers for the fulfillment of your Word that I might pray rightly, that your plans for the future may be achieved for your glory and honor, and the salvation of many. Amen."

4. PRAY WHEN SIGNS INDICATE A BLESSING

4. When the signs of the times, or the providence of God, indicate that *a particular blessing* is about to be bestowed, we are bound to believe it. The Lord Jesus Christ blamed the Jews and called them hypocrites because they did not understand the indications of Providence. They could understand the signs of the weather, and see when it was about to rain and when it would be fair weather; but they could not see, from the signs of the times, that the time had come for the Messiah to appear, and build up the house of God.

There are many professors of religion who are always stumbling and hanging back whenever anything is proposed to be done. They always say, "The time has not come—the time has not come," when there are others who pay attention to the signs of the times, and who have spiritual discernment to understand them. These pray in faith for the blessing, and it comes.

5. When the *Spirit of God is upon you*, and excites strong desires for any blessing, you are bound to pray for it in faith. You are bound to infer, from the fact that you find yourself drawn to desire, such a thing while in the exercise of such holy affections as the Spirit of God produces, that these desires are the work of the Spirit. People are not apt to desire with the right kind of desires unless they are excited by the Spirit of God.

The apostle refers to these desires, excited by the Spirit, in his Epistle to the Romans, where he says: "Likewise the Spirit also helpeth our infirmities: for we know not what we should pray for as we ought: but the Spirit itself maketh intercession for us with groanings which cannot be uttered. And he that searcheth the hearts knoweth what is the mind of the Spirit, because he maketh intercession for the saints according to the will of God" (Rom. 8:26, 27).

If, then, you find yourself strongly drawn to desire a blessing, you are to understand it as an intimation that God is willing to bestow that particular blessing, and so you are bound to believe it. God does not trifle with His children. He does not go and excite in them a desire for one blessing to turn them off with something else. But He excites the very desires He is willing to gratify. And when they feel such desires, they are bound to follow them out till they get the blessing.

Prayer

"Dear God, make me more sensitive to life around me. Help me to face the world and other people with eyes wide open—open to the possibilities of service and salvation through work and prayer that are ever before me. Make me more sensitive to the work and movement of the Holy Spirit in my life that I might know the difference between the groanings of the Spirit and my own feelings of melancholy or depression. Amen."

5. PRAYERS OF FAITH OBTAIN THEIR OBJECT

All the history of the church shows that when God answers prayer He gives His people the very thing for which their prayers are offered. God confers other blessings, on both saints and sinners, which they do not pray for at all. He sends His rain both upon the just and the unjust. But when He *answers prayer*, it is by doing what they ask Him to do. To be sure, He often *more* than answers prayer. He grants them not only what they ask, but often connects other blessings with it.

It is evident that the prayer of faith will obtain the blessing from the fact that our faith rests on evidence that to grant *that* thing is the will of God—not evidence that something else will be granted, but that this particular thing will be. But how, then, can we have evidence that *this* thing will be granted if *another* thing is to be granted? People often receive more than they pray for. Solomon prayed for wisdom, and God granted him riches and honor in addition. So, a wife sometimes prays for the conversion of her husband, and if she offers the prayer of faith, God may not only grant that blessing, but also convert her child and her whole family. Blessings seem sometimes to "hang together," so that if a Christian gains one he gets them all.

Prayer

"O Lord, these words are hard to understand. Help me to more carefully think through what I can pray for in faith before I storm the throne of grace. Help me to carefully

weigh the promises of Scripture and prophetic declarations, the signs of the times, and the groanings of the Spirit that I might pray the prayer of faith based upon the evidence before me. Tell me, Father, when I have failed to pray the prayer of faith, so that I can see more clearly your never-failing answers to my prayers. Amen."

6. HOW TO PRAY A PRAYER OF FAITH

1. *You must first obtain evidence that God will bestow the blessing.* How did Daniel prepare to offer the prayer of faith? He searched the Scriptures. Now, you can not let your Bible lie on a shelf and expect God to reveal His promises to you. "Search the Scriptures" and see where you can get either a general or special promise, or a prophecy, on which you can plant your feet. Go through your Bible, and you will find it full of such precious promises which you may plead in faith.

I could name many individuals who have set themselves to examine the Bible on this subject, who, before they got half through with it, have been filled with the spirit of prayer. They found that God meant by His promises just what a plain, common-sense man would understand them to mean. I advise you to try it. You have Bibles. Search through them, and whenever you find a promise that you can use, fasten it in your mind before you go on. You will not get through the Book without discovering that God's promises mean just what they say.

2. *Cherish the good desires you have.* Christians very often lose their good desires by not attending to this, and then their prayers are mere words, without any desire or earnestness at all. The least longing or desire must be cherished. So if you have the least desire for a blessing, be it ever so small, do not trifle it away. Do not lose good desires by levity, by censoriousness, by worldly-mindedness. Watch and pray.

Prayer

"Lord Jesus, I desire to know your Word, and I long to read it intelligently and apply it to my life. As I pray the prayer of faith, fill me with freshness of your Spirit that I might long to pick up the Scriptures and hear the wonderful words of life. Amen."

7. THE PRAYER OF FAITH
(Continued)

3. *Entire consecration to God is indispensable to the prayer of faith.* You must live a holy life, and consecrate all to God—your time, talents, influence—all you have, all you are, to be His entirely. Read the lives of pious men and you will be struck with the fact that they used to set apart times to renew their covenant and to dedicate themselves anew to God. Whenever they did so, a blessing always followed immediately. If I had President Edwards' works here, I could read passages showing how God answered prayer in answer to complete dedication.

4. *You must persevere.* You are not to pray for a thing once and then cease, and call that the prayer of faith. Look at Daniel. He prayed twenty-one days, and did not cease till he had obtained the blessing. He set his heart and his face unto the Lord, to seek by prayer and supplications, with fasting, and sackcloth, and ashes. He held on for three weeks, and then the answer came. Why didn't it come before? God had sent an archangel to bear the message, but the devil hindered him all this time.

See what Christ says in the parable of the unjust Judge and the parable of the Loaves. What does He teach us by them? Why, that God will grant answers to prayer when it is importunate. "Shall not God avenge his own elect, which *cry day and night unto him?*" (Luke 18:7).

If you would pray in faith, be sure to *walk every day with God.* If you do, He will tell you what to pray for. Be filled with His Spirit, and He will give you objects enough to pray for. He will give you as much of the spirit of prayer as you have strength of body to bear.

Prayer

"O Lord, my God and Savior, I consecrate myself to you, right now, to you and your use—my mind, my heart, my soul, my talents, my time, and my treasures. I dedicate my life to serving you in all ways and to following you wherever you lead. I feel free, O God, knowing that you possess me fully and that you will guide me in the prayers that you desire to answer. Amen."

Sources for "Prayer of Faith"

Definition: *Revivals of Religion*, p. 76.
   1. Ibid., pp. 76, 77.
   2. Ibid., pp. 77-80.
   3. Ibid., pp. 80, 81.
   4. Ibid., pp. 81, 82.
   5. Ibid., pp. 82, 83, 86.
   6. Ibid., pp. 86, 87.
   7. Ibid., p. 88.

The Spirit of Prayer

"How little complaining there is that people do not make enough of the Spirit's influence in leading Christians to pray according to the will of God! Let it never be forgotten that no Christian ever prays aright unless led by the Spirit. He has natural power to pray, and so far as the will of God is revealed, is *able* to do it; but he never does unless the Spirit of God influences him; just as sinners are able to repent, but never do, unless influenced by the Spirit."

1. WHY WE NEED THE HOLY SPIRIT

1. *He intercedes for the saints.* "He maketh intercession for us" and "helpeth our infirmities" when "we know not what to pray for as we ought." He helps Christians to pray "according to the will of God," or for the things that God desires them to pray for.

2. *Because of our ignorance.* Because we know not what we should pray for as we ought. We are so ignorant of the will of God revealed in the Bible, and of His unrevealed will, as we ought to learn it from His providence. People are vastly ignorant both of the promises and prophecies of the Bible, and blind to the providence of God. And they are still more in the dark about those points of which God has said nothing except through the leadings of His Spirit. I have named these four sources of evidence on which to ground faith in prayer—promises, prophecies, providences, and the Holy Spirit. When all other means fail to lead us to the knowledge of what we ought to pray for, the Spirit does it.

3. *He prays for us by exciting our faculties.* Not that He immediately suggests to us words, or guides our language, but He enlightens our minds and makes the truth take hold of our souls. He leads us to a deep consideration of the current issues, of the state of the church, and the condition of sinners. And the natural and philosophical result is deep feeling. When the Spirit brings the truth before a man's mind, there is only one way in which he can keep from deep feeling: by turning away his thoughts and allowing his mind to think of other things.

Prayer

"O God, send the power of the Holy Spirit into my life. Excite me now about what I am to pray for. Lead me to dwell on those things that will overpower my feelings and bring love and compassion for people who need to know of salvation. May I feel a deeper love for the church, and seek to pray for the accomplishment of her mission. Amen."

2. THE HOLY SPIRIT AND SCRIPTURE

It is the Holy Spirit who leads Christians to understand and apply the promises of Scripture. It is wonderful that in no age have Christians been able fully to apply the promises of Scripture to the events of life. This is not because the promises themselves are obscure, but because there has always been an amazing disposition to overlook the Scriptures as a source of light respecting the passing events of life.

How astonished the apostles were at Christ's application of so many prophecies to himself! They seemed to be ready to exclaim continually: "Astonishing! Can it be so? We never understood it before!" Who, that has witnessed the manner in which the apostles, influenced and inspired by the Holy Ghost, applied passages of the Old Testament to Gospel times, has not been amazed at the richness of meaning which they found in the Scriptures? So it has been with many a Christian: while deeply engaged in prayer, he has seen passages of Scriptures he never thought of before as having such appropriate application.

It often happens when professors of religion are praying for their children. Sometimes they pray, and are in darkness and doubt, feeling as if there were no foundation for faith and no special promises for the children of believers. But while they have been pleading, God has shown them the full meaning of some promise, and their soul has rested on it as on His mighty arm.

I once heard of a widow who was greatly exercised about her children until this passage was brought powerfully to her mind: "Thy fatherless children, I will preserve them alive; and let thy widows trust in me" (Jer. 49:11). She saw it had an extended meaning, and she was enabled to lay hold of it, as it were, with her hands. She prevailed in prayer, and her children were converted. The Holy Spirit was sent into the world by the Savior to guide *His people*, to instruct them, and to bring things to their remembrance, as well as to convince the world of sin.

Prayer

"Come Holy Spirit, come as the light of the mind and the fire of the heart. As I immerse myself in the holy Word of God, as I endeavor to apply the promises of God to my life, enlighten me regarding those truths that are hidden from my sight because of my lack of concentration and failing memory. When I bring my troubles and my joys before my Father, share with me the words of life that were written so long ago. Amen."

3. THE HOLY SPIRIT AND SALVATION

The Spirit leads Christians to desire and pray for things of which nothing is specifically said in the Word of God. Take the case of an individual. That God is willing to save is a general truth. So it is a general truth that He is willing to answer prayer. But how shall I know the will of God respecting that individual—whether or not I can pray in faith according to the will of God for the conversion and salvation of the individual? Here the agency of the Spirit comes in to lead the minds of God's people to pray for those individuals, and at those times, when God is prepared to bless them. When we know not what to pray for, the Holy Spirit leads the mind to dwell on some subject, to consider its situation, to realize its value, and to feel for it, and pray, and "travail in birth," till the person is converted.

I was acquainted with an individual who used to keep a list of persons for whom he was especially concerned; and I have had the opportunity to know a multitude of persons, for whom he became thus interested, who were immediately converted. I have seen him pray for persons on his list when he was literally in an agony for them, and have sometimes known him to call on some other person to help him pray for such a one. I have known his mind to fasten thus on an individual of hardened, abandoned character, and who could not be reached in any ordinary way. In this manner the Spirit of God leads individual Christians to pray for things which they would not pray for unless they were led by the Spirit; and thus they pray for things "according to the will of God."

The plain truth of the matter is, that the Spirit leads a man to pray; and if God leads a man to pray for an individual, the inference from the Bible is that God designs to save that individual. If we find, by comparing our state of mind with the Bible, that we are *led by the Spirit* to pray for an individual, we have good evidence to believe that God is prepared to bless him.

Prayer

"Dear Heavenly Father, giver of life and salvation, I pray this day that you would reveal to me by the power of your Holy Spirit a person who is in need of salvation or the healing touch of your loving hand. I do not completely understand the mystery whereby you seek to save others by my prayers and the truth I proclaim, but I do know that you desire to be a co-worker with your children. Amen."

4. THE HOLY SPIRIT AND PROVIDENCE

The Holy Spirit gives to Christians a spiritual discernment respecting the movements and developments of Providence. Devoted, praying Christians often see these things so clearly, and look so far ahead, as to stumble others. They sometimes almost seem to prophesy. No doubt persons may be deluded, and sometimes are, by leaning to their own understanding when they think they are led by the Spirit. But there is no doubt that a Christian may be made to discern clearly the signs of the times, so as to understand, by Providence, what to expect, and thus to pray for it in faith. Thus they are often led to expect a revival, and to pray for it in faith, when nobody else can see the least signs of it.

I'm reminded of a woman in New Jersey, who lived in a place where there had been a revival. She was very positive there was going to be another revival. She wanted to have "conference meetings" scheduled, but the minister and elders saw nothing to encourage it, and would do nothing. Convinced they were blind to the prospect, she went ahead and recruited a carpenter to make seats for her, for she said she would have meetings in her own home; there was certainly going to be a revival. She had scarcely opened her doors for meetings before the Spirit of God came down with great power, and the sleepy church members found themselves surrounded all at once with convicted sinners. They could only say: "Surely the Lord is in this place; and we knew it not" (Gen. 28:16).

The reason why such persons as this praying woman understand the indication of God's will is not because of the superior wisdom that is in them, but because the Spirit of God leads them to see the signs of the times. This is not by revelation but by converging of providences to a single point which produces in them a confident expectation of a certain result.

Prayer

"Dear Father, lead me by the power of your Holy Spirit to see your guiding hand in the daily occurrences of my life and in the daily events of my community and world. Bring revival to my heart, my home, and my church and community. Help me to see signs of that revival. May I be willing to do what is necessary, despite opposition, that I might lead others to commitment to, and knowledge of, Jesus Christ. Amen."

5. DISTINGUISHING THE HOLY SPIRIT

We are not to expect to feel our minds in direct physical contact with God. If such a thing can be, we know of no way in which it can be made sensible. We know that we exercise our minds freely, and that our thoughts are exercised on something that excites our feelings. But we are not to expect a miracle to be wrought, as if we were led by the hand, sensibly, or as if something whispered in the ear, or any miraculous manifestation of the will of God.

Individuals often grieve the Spirit away because they do not harbor Him and cherish His influence. Sinners often do this ignorantly. They suppose that if they were under conviction by the Spirit, they should have such-and-such mysterious feelings—a shock would come upon them which they could not mistake.

Many Christians are so ignorant of the Spirit's influences, and have thought so little about having His assistance in prayer, that when they have such influences they do not know it, and so do not yield to them, and cherish them. We are sensing nothing in the case—only the movements of our own minds. There is nothing else that *can* be felt. We are merely sensing that our thoughts are intensely employed on a certain subject.

Christians are often unnecessarily misled and distressed on this point for fear they have not the Spirit of God. They feel intensely, but they know not what makes them feel. They are distressed about sinners; but should they not be distressed when they think of their condition? They keep thinking about them all the time. And why should they not be distressed? Now the truth is, that the very fact that you are *thinking* upon them is evidence that the Spirit of God is leading you.

Do you not know that the greater part of the time these things do not affect you so? The greater part of the time you do not think much about the case of sinners. You know their salvation is always equally important. But at other times, even when you are quite at leisure, your mind is entirely dark and vacant of any feeling for them.

But now, although you may be busy about other things, you think, you pray, and feel intensely for them, even while you are about business that at other times would occupy all your thoughts. Now, almost every thought you have is: "God, have mercy upon them!" Why is this? Because their case is placed in a strong light before your mind.

Do you ask what it is that leads your mind to exercise benevolent feelings for sinners and to agonize in prayer for them? What can it be but the Spirit of God? There are no devils that would lead you so. If your feelings are truly benevolent, you are to consider it as the Holy Spirit leading you to pray for things according to the will of God.

Prayer

"Dear Heavenly Father, quite often I have expected you to do more than is necessary to convince me that I am in possession of your Holy Spirit, or rather, that your Holy Spirit is in possession of me. Help me to channel my thoughts and my feelings along constructive paths, making me ever concerned about building up your kingdom and ministering to the lost. By loving thoughts and actions, enable me to distinguish the Spirit in my life. Amen."

6. DISTINGUISHING THE SPIRIT
(Continued)

"Try the spirits" by the Bible. People are sometimes led away by strange fantasies and crazy impulses. If you compare them faithfully with the Bible, you never need to be led astray. You can always know whether your feelings are produced by the Spirit's influences by comparing your desires with the spirit and temper of religion, as described in the Bible. The Bible commands you to "try the spirits." "Beloved, believe not every spirit, but try the spirits whether they are of God" (1 John 4:1).

There is a class of minds, that in seasons of deep excitement, and especially when there is a good deal of preaching on the necessity and reality of divine influences, the spirit of prayer, being led by the Spirit, being filled with the Spirit, etc., who are extremely apt to give themselves up to be led by impulses. They mistake the true manner in which the Spirit of God influences the mind, not realizing that He enlightens the intelligence, and leads the Christian who is under His influence to be eminently reasonable and rational in all his views and movements. They look for the Spirit to make direct impressions on their feelings and not through the intelligence. Hence they are full of impressions.

Satan often succeeds by transforming himself into an angel of light, in persuading them to give themselves up to impulses and impressions; and from that moment, he leads them captive at his will.

I remark that, as a general rule, the influence of Satan in these things may be distinguished from the influences of the Holy Spirit by this: a mere impression that you must do this or that thing, go and converse with this person or that person, go to this place or that place. This is by no means to be regarded. When the Spirit of God leads an individual to take a peculiar interest, feel peculiar compassion and drawing of heart in prayer and labor for particular individuals, this influence may be safely trusted.

If you find yourself drawn out in mighty prayer for certain individuals, exercised with great compassion, agonized with strong crying and tears, for a certain family or neighborhood or people, let such an influence be yielded to.

Prayer

"Lord Jesus, sometimes I am selfish, wanting to experience things for their own sake, wanting to feel the Spirit in order to feel good, reassure myself of salvation, or guide me to some exotic place or person. Help me to be directed toward the needs of the other people in my life and world. Help me to feel love and compassion for the physically and spiritually needy. Help me find intelligent and loving ways to meet these needs, and then I will know I am led by the Spirit. Amen."

7. TO RECEIVE THE SPIRIT'S INFLUENCE

The Holy Spirit must be sought by fervent, believing prayer. Christ says: "If ye then, being evil, know how to give good gifts unto your children; how much more shall your heavenly Father give the Holy Spirit to them that ask him?" (Luke 11:13).

Does anyone say, "I have prayed for it, and it does not come"? It is because you do not pray aright. "Ye ask, and receive not, because ye ask amiss, that ye may consume it upon your lusts" (James 4:3). You do not pray from right motives.

A professor of religion, and a principal member in a church, once asked a minister what he thought of his case. He had been praying week after week for the Spirit, and had not found any benefit. The minister asked what his motive was in praying. He replied that he "wanted to be happy." He knew those who had the Spirit were happy, and he wanted to enjoy his mind as they did. Why, the devil himself might pray so! That is mere selfishness.

Use the means adopted to stir up your minds on the subject and to keep your attention fixed there. If a man prays for the Spirit and then diverts his mind to other objects, he tempts God, he swings loose from his object, and it would be a miracle if he should get what he prays for. God is not going to pour these things on you without any effort of your own.

You must watch unto prayer. You must keep a lookout and see if God grants the blessing when you ask Him. People sometimes pray but never look to see if the prayer is granted.

Be careful, also, not to grieve the Spirit of God. Confess and forsake your sins. God will never lead you as one of His hidden ones and let you into His secrets unless you confess and forsake your sins. Be not always confessing and never forsaking, but confess and forsake, too. Make redress wherever you have committed an injury.

Aim to obey perfectly the written law. In other words, have no fellowship with sin. Aim at being entirely above the world: "Be ye therefore perfect, even as your Father which is in heaven is perfect" (Matt. 5:48). If you sin at all, let it be your daily grief. The man who does not aim at this, means to live in sin. Such a man need not expect God's blessing, for he is not sincere in desiring to keep all His commandments.

Prayer

"Come Holy Spirit, abide in my life and influence me with your quiet stirrings of the mind and the heart. I confess that I have desired to know you for self-centered reasons, and I forsake now all selfish desire for you. I ask only that I may know you to glorify Jesus Christ in my life, and that I may lead others to come to know and accept the way of salvation. Amen."

8. PRAYER AND THE CHURCH

There are three classes of persons in the church who are liable to error, or have left the truth out of view, on this subject.

1. Those who place great reliance on prayer, and use no other means. They are alarmed at any special means, and talk about your "getting up a revival."

2. Those who use means, and pray, but never think about the influences of the Spirit in prayer. They talk about prayer for the Spirit, and feel the importance of the Spirit in the conversion of sinners, but do not realize the importance of the Spirit in prayer. And their prayers are all cold talk—nothing that anybody can feel or that can take hold of God.

3. Those who have certain strange notions about the sovereignty of God, and are waiting for God to convert the world without prayer or means.

Now, will you give yourselves up to prayer and live so as to have the spirit of prayer and have the Spirit with you all the time? Oh, for a praying church! I once knew a minister who had a revival fourteen winters in succession. I did not know how to account for it till I saw one of his members get up in a prayer meeting and make a confession. "Brethren," said he, "I have been long in the habit of praying every Saturday night till after midnight for the descent of the Holy Ghost among us. And now, brethren," and he began to weep, "I confess that I have neglected it for two or three weeks." The secret was out. That minister had a praying church.

Brethren, in my present state of health, I find it impossible to pray as much as I have been in the habit of doing and yet continue to preach. It overcomes my strength. Now, shall I give myself up to prayer and stop preaching? That will not do. Now, will not you, who are in health, throw yourselves into this work, bear this burden, and give yourselves to prayer till God shall pour out His blessing upon us?

Prayer

"Dear God, holy, loving, and merciful, I desire to pray rightly with all my heart. There is much that I must learn and digest if my prayers are going to be as effective as they can be. I know you hear even the feeble prayer of the sinner, but still great power for revival and the spread of the Gospel must come from the intelligent, Spirit-influenced prayers of the saints. May I pray the prayer of the saint, and not the feeble sinner, that your kingdom may come on this earth as it is in heaven. Amen."

Sources for "The Spirit of Prayer"

Definition: *Revivals of Religion*, p. 106.
1. Ibid., pp. 94, 95, 96.
2. Ibid., pp. 96, 98.
3. Ibid., pp. 98-100.
4. Ibid., pp. 100, 101.
5. Ibid., pp. 102, 103.
6. Ibid., p. 103 and *Reflections on Revival*, pp. 64, 65.
7. Ibid., pp. 103-106.
8. Ibid., pp. 112-114.

Be Filled with the Spirit

"I wish to show that, if you live without the Spirit, you are without excuse. Obligation to perform duty never rests on the condition that we shall have the influence of the Spirit, but on the powers of moral agency. We, as moral agents, have the power to obey God, and are perfectly bound to obey; and the reason that we do not is that we are unwilling."

1. YOU MAY AND MUST HAVE THE SPIRIT

You must have the Spirit, not because it is a matter of justice for God to give you His Spirit, but because *He has promised* to give His Spirit to those that ask. "If ye then, being evil, know how to give good gifts unto your children: *how much more* shall your heavenly Father give the Holy Spirit to them that ask him?" (Luke 11:13). If you ask for the Holy Spirit, God has promised to answer.

But again, *God has commanded* you to have the Spirit. He says in the text, "Be filled with the Spirit" (Eph. 5:18). When God commands us to do a thing, it is the highest possible evidence that we can do it. For God to command is equivalent to an oath that we can do it. He has no right to command unless we have the power to obey. There is no stopping short of the conclusion that God is tyrannical if He commands that which is impracticable.

It is your *duty to be filled with the Spirit.*

It is your duty because you have a promise of it. God has commanded it.

It is essential to your own growth in grace that you should be filled with the Spirit.

It is as important as it is that you should be sanctified.

It is as necessary as it is that you should be useful and do good in the world.

If you do not have the Spirit of God in you, you will dishonor God, disgrace the church, and be lost.

Prayer

"Dear Heavenly Father, I tend to take my faith for granted. I don't understand the importance of the gifts that you want to bestow upon me for the sake of your kingdom and my salvation. I know that you want me as a co-worker with you, and I am overwhelmed and humbled by that honor and responsibility. Over these next few days, guide me and fill me that I may be of holy service to you by the power of the Spirit. Amen."

2. WHAT PREVENTS YOUR BEING FILLED

1. It may be that you live a hypocritical life. Your prayers are not earnest and sincere. Not only is your religion a mere outside show, without any heart, but you are insincere in your intercourse with others. Thus you do many things to grieve the Spirit so that He cannot dwell with you.

2. Others have so much levity that the Spirit will not dwell with them. The Spirit of God is solemn, and serious, and will not dwell with those who give way to thoughtless levity.

3. Others are so proud that they cannot have the Spirit. They are so fond of dress, high life, equipage, fashion, etc., that it is no wonder they are not filled with the Spirit. And yet such persons will pretend to be at a loss to know why it is that they do not "enjoy" religion!

4. Some are so worldly-minded, love property so well, and are trying so hard to get rich that they cannot have the Spirit. How can He dwell with them when all their thoughts are on things of the world and all their powers absorbed in procuring wealth? And when they get money, they are pained if pressed by conscience to do something with it for the conversion of the world.

5. Others do not *fully* confess and *forsake* their sins, and so cannot enjoy the Spirit's presence. They will confess their sins in general terms, perhaps, and are ready always to acknowledge that they are sinners. But they do it reservedly, proudly, guardedly, as if they were afraid they

should say a little more than is necessary—that is, when they confess to men.

6. Others are neglecting some known duty, and that is the reason why they have not the Spirit. If you have neglected any known duty, and thus lost the spirit of prayer, you must yield first. God has a controversy with you. God never will yield or grant you His Spirit till you repent.

7. Perhaps you have resisted the Spirit of God. Perhaps you are in the *habit* of resisting the Spirit. You resist conviction. Many are willing to hear plain and searching preaching so long as they can apply it all to other people.

8. The fact is that you do not, *on the whole*, desire the Spirit. This is true in every case in which people do not have the Spirit. Nothing is more common than for people to desire a thing on some accounts which they do not choose *on the whole*.

9. Perhaps you do not pray for the Spirit; or you pray and use no other means, or pray and do not act consistently with your prayers. Or you use means calculated to resist them. Or you ask, and as soon as He comes and begins to affect your mind, you grieve Him right away and will not walk with Him.

Prayer

"O God, may I take the time to examine myself and my motives for conduct and desire for the Spirit. There are many things that I may not be willing to give up for the Spirit, and so I am blind to these faults that grieve the Spirit of God away. Shine the light of your truth upon my life as I attend to public worship, Scripture reading, prayer and service. Alert my conscience that I might see what is keeping me spiritually empty, and strengthen me as I willingly try to conform my life to your will. Amen."

3. RESULTS OF BEING FILLED

You will be called eccentric if you are filled with the Spirit—and probably you will deserve it. Probably you will really be eccentric. I never knew a person who was filled with the Spirit that was not called eccentric. And the reason is that such people are unlike other folk.

There is therefore the best of reasons why such people should appear eccentric. They act under different influences, take different views, are moved by different motives, led by a different spirit. You are to expect such remarks.

There is such a thing as affected eccentricity. Horrible! But there is such a thing as being deeply imbued with the Spirit of God that you must and will act so as to appear strange and eccentric to those who cannot understand the reasons of your conduct.

If you have much of the Spirit of God, it is likely you will be thought deranged by many. We judge men to be deranged when they act differently from what we think to be according to prudence and common sense, and when they come to conclusions for which we can see no good reasons. Multitudes have appeared, to those who had no spirituality, as if they were deranged. Yet *they* saw good reasons for doing as they did. God was leading their minds to act in such a way that those who were not spiritual could not see the reasons.

If you have the Spirit of God, you must expect to feel great distress in view of the condition of the church and of the world. Some spiritual epicures ask for the Spirit because they think He will make them so perfectly happy.

Some people think that spiritual Christians are always free from sorrow. There never was a greater mistake.

Read your Bibles and see how the prophets and apostles were always groaning and distressed in view of the state of the church and of the world. The Apostle Paul says he was "always bearing about in the body the dying of the Lord Jesus" (2 Cor. 4:10). "I protest," says he, "I die daily" (1 Cor. 15:31).

You will know what it is to sympathize with the Lord Jesus Christ and be baptized with the baptism that He was baptized with. The more you have of His Spirit, the more clearly will you see the state of sinners, and the more deeply you will be distressed about them.

Prayer

"Lord Jesus, may I not be afraid but ask boldly for the outpouring of the Holy Spirit into my life. May I not be afraid or shrink from accusations or ridicule of others but be willing to stand up for your kingdom. Help me to see clearly and know that the Spirit will lead me into greater wisdom and love, even though your wisdom and love may appear as foolishness to the world. Amen."

4. RESULTS OF BEING FILLED
(Continued)

If you have much of the Spirit of God, you must make up your mind to have much opposition, both in the church and the world. Very likely the leading men in the church will oppose you. So it was when Christ was on earth. If you are far above their state of feeling, church members will oppose you. "All that will live godly in Christ Jesus shall suffer persecution" (2 Tim. 3:12). Often the elders, and even the minister, will oppose you if you are filled with the Spirit of God.

You must expect very frequent and agonizing conflicts with Satan. Satan has very little trouble with those Christians who are not spiritual, but lukewarm, and slothful, and worldly-minded. And such do not understand what is said about spiritual conflicts.

But spiritual Christians, he understands very well, are doing him a vast injury; therefore he sets himself against them. Such Christians often have terrible conflicts. They have temptations that they never thought of before: blasphemous thoughts, atheism, suggestions to do deeds of wickedness, to destroy their own lives, and the like. And if you are spiritual, you may expect these terrible conflicts.

You will have greater conflicts with yourself than you ever thought of. You will sometimes find your own corruptions making strange headway against the Spirit. "The flesh lusteth against the Spirit, and the Spirit against the flesh" (Gal. 5:17). Such a Christian is often thrown into consternation at the power of his own corruptions.

Prayer

"Dear Heavenly Father, my expectations of the Christian life were so radically different from what I experienced once I began to take you seriously that I was confused and doubted the substance of my faith. Help me to pray for those who oppose me, and enable me to keep silent, except where motivated by a spirit of love and intelligence. May I not strike out at others because Satan is striking out at me. Amen."

5. THE STATE OF THE MINISTRY

You will be often grieved with the state of the ministry. Some years ago I met a woman belonging to one of the churches in this city. I inquired of her the state of religion here. She seemed unwilling to say much about it, made some general remarks, and then choked, and her eyes filled, and she said: "Oh, our minister's mind seems to be very dark!"

Spiritual Christians often feel like this, and often weep over it. I have seen much of it, having found Christians who wept and groaned in secret, to see the darkness in the minds of ministers in regard to religion, the earthliness, and fear of man; but they dared not speak of it lest they should be denounced and threatened, and perhaps turned out of the church.

I do not say these things censoriously to reproach my brethren, but because they are true. And ministers ought to know that nothing is more common than for spiritual Christians to feel burdened and distressed at the state of the ministry.

This is one of the most prominent and deeply-to-be-deplored evils of the present day. The *piety* of the ministry, though *real*, is so superficial, in many instances, that the spiritual people of the church feel that ministers do not, cannot, sympathize with them. The preaching does not meet their wants; it does not feed them. The ministers have not depth enough of religious experience to know how to search and wake up the church—how to help those under temptation, to support the weak, to direct the strong.

When a minister has gone with a church as far as his experience in spiritual exercises goes, there he stops. And until he has a renewed experience, until he is reconverted, his heart broken up afresh, and he set forward in the divine life and Christian experience, he will help them no more.

He may preach sound doctrine—and so may an unconverted minister—but, after all, his preaching will want that searching pungency, that practical bearing, that unction which alone will reach the case of a spiritually-minded Christian.

It is a fact over which the church is groaning, that the piety of young men suffers so much in the course of their education, that when they enter the ministry, however much intellectual furniture they may possess, they are in a state of *spiritual babyhood.* They want nursing; they need to be fed rather than to undertake to feed the church of God.

Ministers often groan and struggle and wear themselves out in vain, trying to do good where there is a people who live so that they do not have the Spirit of God. If the Spirit is poured out at any time, the church will grieve Him right away. Thus, you may tie the hands and break the heart of your minister, and break him down, and perhaps kill him, because you are not filled with the Spirit.

Prayer

"Lord Jesus, I grieve over the state of the ministry, the laity, and the church, wherever there is spiritual deadness and apathy. I particularly pray for the ministry, a converted ministry, that will preach the Gospel of Jesus Christ because it is true, and pray for the outpouring and influence of the Holy Spirit in the lives of every person to make the truth effective. May the ministry be characterized by a devout and holy life, as an example to the Christian and the unconverted. Amen."

6. THE BLESSINGS OF BEING FILLED

1. You will have peace with God. If the church, and sinners, and the devil, oppose you, there will be One with whom you will have peace. Let you who are called to these trials, and conflicts, and temptations, and who groan, pray, weep, and break your hearts, remember this consideration: your peace, so far as your feelings towards God are concerned, will flow like a river.

2. You will likewise have peace of conscience if you are led by the Spirit. You will not be constantly goaded and kept on the rack by a guilty conscience. Your conscience will be calm and quiet, unruffled as the summer's lake.

3. If filled with the Spirit, you will be useful. You cannot help being useful. Even if you were sick and unable to go out of your room, or to converse, and saw nobody, you would be ten times more useful than a hundred of those common sort of Christians who have no spirituality.

To give you an idea of this, I will relate an anecdote. A pious man in the western part of this state was suffering from consumption. He was a poor man and was ill for years. An unconverted merchant in the place, who had a kind heart, used to send him, now and then, some things for his comfort or for his family. He felt grateful for the kindness but could make no return as he wanted to do.

At length he determined that the best return he could make would be to pray, and his soul kindled, and he got hold of God. No revival was taking place there, but, by and by, to the astonishment of everybody, this merchant came right out on the Lord's side. The fire kindled all over the place; and powerful revival followed, and multitudes were converted.

4. If you are filled with the Spirit, you will not find yourselves distressed, and galled, and worried when people speak against you.

5. You will be wise in using means for the conversion of sinners. If the Spirit of God is in you, He will lead you to use means wisely, in a way adapted to the end, and to avoid doing hurt.

6. You will be calm under affliction, not thrown into confusion or consternation when you see the storm coming over you.

7. You will be resigned in death; you will always feel prepared to die and not afraid to die; and after death you will be proportionately more happy forever in heaven.

Prayer

"O Lord Most High, fill me with your Holy Spirit. I come not with selfish reasons but with a real desire to glorify you and your Son Jesus Christ. My life is often in turmoil and in affliction; but I know that through the presence of your Spirit, I can be a calm and steadfast witness to the peace which passes understanding. In Jesus' Name and for His sake, Amen."

7. EFFECTS OF SPIRITUAL EMPTINESS

1. You will often doubt, in such a case, and reasonably so, whether you are a Christian. You will have doubts, and you ought to have them, for the sons of God are led by the Spirit of God, and if you are not led by the Spirit, what reason have you to think that you are a son?

2. You will always be unsettled in your views about the prayer of faith. The prayer of faith is something so spiritual, so much a matter of experience and not of speculation, that unless you are spiritual yourselves you will not understand it fully.

3. If you have not the Spirit, you will be very apt to stumble at those who have. You will doubt the propriety of their conduct. If they seem to feel a good deal more than yourself, you will be likely to call it "animal feeling." You will perhaps doubt their sincerity when they say they have such feelings.

4. You will have a good reputation with the impenitent and with carnal professors. They will praise you as "a rational, orthodox, consistent Christian." You will be just in the frame of mind to walk with them because you are agreed.

5. You will be much troubled with fears about fanaticism. Whenever there are revivals, you will see in them "a strong tendency to fanaticism," and will be full of fears and anxiety.

6. You will be much disturbed by the measures that are used in revivals. If any measures are adopted, that are de-

cided and direct, you will think they are all "New," and will stumble at them just in proportion to your want of spirituality.

7. You will be a reproach to religion. The impenitent will sometimes praise you because you are so much like themselves, and sometimes laugh about you because you are such a hypocrite.

8. You will know but little about the Bible.

9. If you die without the Spirit, you will fall into hell. There can be no doubt about this. Without the Spirit you will never be prepared for heaven.

Prayer

"Lord, I pray for that Christian, spiritual consistency that is the fruit of being filled with your Spirit. Some of the effects of spiritual emptiness I find in my life now, and I know that they can be remedied only by my desire for and your gift of the power of the Holy Spirit in my life. I commit my life anew to you now, and await for the spiritual awakening that will take place as I learn and practice your truth in my daily life. Amen."

8. NECESSITY OF DIVINE INFLUENCE

I have thought that, at least in a great many instances, stress enough has not been laid upon the necessity of divine influence upon the hearts of Christians and of sinners. I am confident that I have sometimes erred in this respect myself.

In order to rout sinners and backsliders from their self-justifying pleas and refuges, I have laid, and I doubt not that others also have laid too much stress upon the natural ability of sinners to the neglect of showing them the nature and extent of their dependence upon the grace of God and the influence of His Spirit.

This has grieved the Spirit of God. His work not being honored by being made sufficiently prominent, and not being able to get the glory to himself of His own work, He has withheld His influences. In the meantime, multitudes have been greatly excited by the means used to promote an excitement, and have obtained hopes, without ever knowing the necessity of the presence and powerful agency of the Holy Ghost. It hardly need be said that such hopes are better thrown away than kept. It were strange indeed if one could lead a Christian life upon the foundation of an experience in which the Holy Ghost is not recognized as having anything to do.

Until the leaders enter into the work, until the ministers are baptized with the Holy Spirit, until we are awake and in the field with our armor on, and our souls anointed with the Holy Spirit, it certainly ill becomes us to be looking around at a distance for the cause of the decline of revivals.

Prayer

"O Lord, the weight of the necessity of spiritual influence in my life, and in others, is upon me. I desire to preach, with real power, release to the captives. However, I know now that there can be no release apart from the anointing influence of your Holy Spirit. May no person's future or eternal salvation be hindered because of my lack of prayer or my failure to ask that my words be guided by your Spirit in the presentation and reception of the truth. Amen."

9. TRUE CHRISTIANITY

Now these dear souls do not realize that there is such a thing as great spiritual activity and aggressiveness, and that true spirituality always implies this: that true faith always begets sympathy with Christ, and that true Christianity is always and necessarily the spirit of missions, of revivals, of self-sacrifice, of holy activity; that it is a living, energizing principle; that holiness in man is just what it was in Christ; indeed, that holiness is always one and the same thing—benevolence or good-willing, and by a law of its own nature is continually putting forth efforts to realize the great end of benevolence—the highest good of all beings. True Christianity is the law of love written in the heart by the Holy Spirit, and, of course, necessarily acted out in practical life.

The mistake of the Antinomians is they do not distinguish between that faith which consists in a persuasion of the intellect, accompanied by a corresponding state of feeling, without assent of the heart or will, and that faith in which the heart or will most fully yields to perceived and admitted truth. The faith of the heart is necessarily a powerful and active principle.

The manner in which they expect, and profess, to be led by the Spirit seems to be that of impulse rather than divine illumination through the Word. They sometimes seem to suppose that the Spirit leads the people of God by impressions upon their sensibility or feelings, rather than by enlightening their intelligence and leading them to act rationally and in accordance with the written Word.

True religion does not consist in obeying ou
but in conforming our heart to the law of our inte.
God has given us reason, and requires us to unde.
what we are about. He has given us the written Word
the Holy Spirit to shine upon it to make us understand i
great principles and the application of them to all the circumstances and duties of life.

A true Christian is active, but his activity and energy
arise out of a deep sympathy with the indwelling Spirit of
Christ. Christ is formed within him. The Spirit of Christ is
the mighty energizing power of his soul.

Prayer

"Come Holy Spirit, convict me of laziness in seeking
your will through the Word you inspired. Forgive me for
testing my feelings for some mysterious sensibility of you,
while neglecting to reasonably think through and apply the
will of God as expressed in the Scriptures to my life here
and now. May I continue to approach true Christianity that
my life may be a witness to others. Amen."

Sources for "Be Filled with the Spirit"

Definition: *Revivals of Religion*, p. 115.
1. Ibid., pp. 116, 117.
2. Ibid., pp. 117-123.
3. Ibid., pp. 124, 125.
4. Ibid., pp. 127, 128.
5. Ibid., pp. 126, 127, 134.
6. Ibid., pp. 128-131.
7. Ibid., pp. 131-133.
8. *Reflections on Revival*, pp. 17, 18, 70.
9. Ibid., pp. 24-26.

Meeting for Prayer

"Hitherto, in treating of the subject of prayer, I have confined my remarks to secret prayer. I am now to speak of social prayer, or prayer offered in company, where two or more are united in praying. Such meetings have been common from the time of Christ, and it is probable that God's people have always been in the habit of making united supplication whenever they had the privilege."

1. PURPOSE OF PUBLIC PRAYER

1. One design of assembling several persons together for united prayer is to *promote union* among Christians. Nothing tends more to cement the hearts of Christians than praying together. Never do they love one another so well as when they witness the outpouring of each other's hearts in prayer.

2. Public prayer enables believers to *extend the spirit of prayer*. God has so constituted us, and such is the economy of His grace, that we are sympathetic beings and communicate our feelings to one another. Nothing is more calculated to beget a spirit of prayer than to unite in social prayer with one who has the spirit himself, unless this one should be so far ahead that his prayer will repel the rest. His prayer will awaken them, if they are not so far behind as to revolt at it and resist it.

3. Another grand design of social prayer is *to move God*. Not that it changes the mind and feelings of God. But when the right kind of prayer is offered by Christians, they are in such a state of mind that it becomes proper for God to bestow a blessing.

4. Another important design of prayer meetings is the *conviction and conversion of sinners*. When properly conducted they are eminently calculated to produce this effect. Sinners are apt to be solemn when they hear Christians pray. Where there is a spirit of prayer, sinners must feel. Just as soon as Christians begin to pray as they ought, sinners then know that they pray and begin to feel awful. They do not understand what spirituality is because they have no

experience of it. When Christians pray in faith, the Spirit of God is poured out, and sinners are melted down and converted on the spot.

Prayer

"Dear Heavenly Father, may I find a way for group prayer in my life. May I find two or three of like mind to pray with in covenant, for each other and the growth of your kingdom. May we be changed to be able and willing to accept the blessings you would bestow, and may we find others to share this joy of faith in your Son Jesus Christ, the Savior of the world. Amen."

2. HOW TO CONDUCT PUBLIC PRAYER

It is often well to open a prayer meeting by *reading a short portion* of the Word of God, especially if the person who leads the meeting can call to mind any portion that will be applicable to the object or occasion that is impressive and to the point.

Do not drag in the Word of God to make up part of the meeting as a mere matter of form. This is an insult to God. It is not well to read any more than is applicable to the subject. The design of the prayer meeting should be to bring Christians to the point, to pray for a definite object. Wandering over a large field hinders and destroys this design.

It is proper that the person who leads should make some short and appropriate remarks calculated to explain the nature of prayer, and the encouragements we have to pray, and to *bring the object to be prayed for* directly before the minds of the people. After stating the object, he should bring up some promise or some principle as the ground of encouragement to expect an answer to their prayers. If there is any indication of Providence, or any promise, or any principle in the divine government that affords a ground of faith, let him call it to mind.

Give up the meeting to the Spirit of God. Those who desire to pray, let them pray. If the leader sees anything that needs to be set right, let him remark freely and kindly and put it right, and then go on again.

If it is necessary to name the individuals who are to pray, it is best to call *first* on those who are *most spiritual*;

if you do not know who they are, then choose those whom you would naturally suppose to be most "alive."

The prayers should be very short. Each one should pray for *some one object*. If, in the progress of the meeting, it becomes necessary to *change the object* of prayer, let the leader state the fact and explain it in a few words. It is important that *the time should be fully occupied* so as not to leave seasons of silence, which make a bad impression and chill the meeting.

It is exceedingly important that he who leads the meeting should press sinners who may be present to *immediate repentance*. He should earnestly urge the Christians who are present to pray in such a way as to make sinners feel that they are expected to repent immediately. This tends to inspire Christians with compassion and love for souls.

Prayer

"O Lord, I often pray in the privacy of my bedroom or office, but I long for group prayer and a means of praying as a group for particular blessings. Please show me a Christian people of like mind, and enable me to begin with these principles in the faith that you will honor them now even as you did in the past. Amen."

3. HINDRANCES TO PUBLIC PRAYER

When there is an unhappy *want of confidence* in the leader, there is no hope of any good. Whatever may be the cause, whether he is to blame or not, the very fact that *he* leads the meeting will cast a damp over it and prevent all good.

Where the leader *lack spirituality*, there will be a dryness and coldness in his remarks and prayers; everything will indicate his want of unction, and his whole influence will be the very reverse of what it ought to be. There may be a want of *suitable talents* in the leader. A man may be pious but so weak that his prayers do not edify but rather disgust.

Sometimes the benefit of a prayer meeting is defeated by a *bad spirit* in the leader. For instance, where there is a revival, and great opposition, if a leader gets up in a prayer meeting and speaks of instances of opposition, and comments upon them, and thus diverts the meeting away from the object, he knows not what spirit he is of. Its effect is always ruinous of a prayer meeting. Let a minister in a revival come out and preach against the opposition, and he will infallibly destroy the revival and turn the hearts of Christians away from their proper object.

Persons *coming late* to meeting make *cold prayers* and cold confessions of sin, and are sure to quench the spirit of prayer.

In some places it is common to begin a prayer meeting by reading *a long portion* of Scripture. Then the deacon or elder gives out a long hymn. Next, they sing it. Then he prays a long prayer, praying for the Jews, and the fullness of the Gentiles, and many other objects that have nothing to do with the occasion of the meeting. After that perhaps he reads a long extract from some book or magazine. Then they have another long hymn and another long prayer and then they go home.

Nothing of a controversial nature should be introduced into a prayer unless it is the object of the meeting to *settle that thing.* Great pains should be taken, both by the leader and others, to *watch narrowly the leadings of the Spirit of God.* Let them not quench the Spirit for the sake of praying according to the regular custom.

If individuals *refuse to pray when they are called upon,* it injures a prayer meeting. Prayer meetings are often *too long.* They should be dismissed while Christians have feeling and not be spun out until all feeling is exhausted. Injury is also done when Christians spend all the time in *praying for themselves.* They should have done this in their own homes. When they come to a prayer meeting, they should be prepared to offer effectual intercessions for others.

A *want of union* in prayer mars the meeting; that is, when one leads but the others do not follow, for they are thinking of something else. Their hearts do not unite and say, "Amen."

Neglect of secret prayer is yet another hindrance. Christians who do not pray in secret cannot unite with power in a prayer meeting and cannot have the spirit of prayer.

Prayer

"Dear Father, there is much to learn about prayer. There are many helpful principles and many dangerous pitfalls as well. May I not be so concerned with the "letter of the law" in my prayers but with the "spirit of the law" that great effectual prayer may be wrought in my life as well as in the lives and purposes of the people who pray with me. Amen."

4. THE NECESSITY OF PUBLIC PRAYER

A prayer meeting is an index to the state of religion in a church. If the prayer meeting is neglected, or the spirit of prayer is not manifested, you know, of course, that religion is in a low condition. Let me go into the prayer meeting, and I can always see the state of religion which prevails in the church.

Every minister ought to know that if the prayer meetings are neglected, all his labors are in vain. Unless he can get Christians to attend the prayer meetings, all else that he can do will not improve the state of religion.

A great responsibility rests on him who leads a prayer meeting. If the meeting be not what it ought to be, if it does not elevate the state of religion, he should go seriously to work and see what is the matter, and get the spirit of prayer, and prepare himself to make such remarks as are calculated to do good and set things right. A leader has no business to lead prayer meetings if he is not prepared, both in head and heart, to do this.

Prayer meetings are most important meetings for the church. It is highly important for Christians to sustain the prayer meetings in order to (a) promote union, (b) increase brotherly love, (c) cultivate Christian confidence, (d) promote their own growth in grace, and (e) cherish and advance spirituality.

Prayer meetings should be so numerous in the church, and be so arranged, as to exercise the gifts of every member—man or woman. Everyone should have the opportunity to pray and to express the feelings of his heart. The sectional prayer meetings are designed to do this. And if they are too large to allow it, let them be divided so as to bring the entire mass into the work, to exercise all gifts, and diffuse union, confidence, and brotherly love, through the whole.

Prayer

"Dear Heavenly Father, if there is no prayer meeting in my church, let it begin with me. I pray that my minister and leaders in my church may see the need of some type of coming together for prayer. Perhaps, O Lord, others have been waiting for me to come forward and propose a weekly time of prayer. Open the hearts of my Christian friends, and open their minds to such a proposal. Show me the way to begin this ministry for the spread of your Gospel. Amen."

Sources for "Meeting for Prayer"

Definition: *Revivals of Religion*, p. 136.
1. Ibid., pp. 136-168.
2. Ibid., pp. 139-142.
3. Ibid., pp. 143-151.
4. Ibid., pp. 151-153.

APPENDIX

The Principles Born of Prayer from *Charles G. Finney, an Autobiography*

When I first went to New York, I had made up my mind on the question of slavery, and was exceedingly anxious to arouse public attention to the subject (1832). I did not, however, turn aside to make it a hobby, or divert the attention of the people from the work of converting souls. Nevertheless, in my prayers and preaching, I so often alluded to slavery, and denounced it, that a considerable excitement came to exist among the people.

As the excitement increased on the subject of slavery, Mr. Leavitt espoused the cause of the slave, and advocated it in the New York *Evangelist*. I watched the discussion with a good deal of attention and anxiety, and when I was about to leave on the sea voyage to which I have referred [Finney took a sea voyage in early 1834 to the Mediterranean on account of his health], I admonished Mr. Leavitt to be careful and not go too fast in the discussion of the anti-slavery question, lest he should destroy his paper.

On my homeward passage, my mind became exceedingly exercised on the question of revivals. I feared that they would decline throughout the country. I feared that the opposition that had been made to them had grieved the Holy Spirit. My own health, it appeared to me, had nearly or quite broken down; and I knew of no other evangelist that would take the field and aid pastors in revival work.

This view of the subject distressed me so much that one day I found myself unable to rest. My soul was in an utter agony. I spent almost the entire day in prayer in my state-room, or walking the deck in intense agony, in view of the state of things. In fact, I felt crushed with the burden that was on my soul. There was no one on board to whom I could open my mind or say a word.

It was the spirit of prayer that was upon me; that which I had often before experienced in kind, but perhaps never before to such a degree, for so long a time. I besought the Lord to go on with His work and to provide himself with such instrumentalities as were necessary. It was a long summer day, in the early part of July.

After a day of unspeakable wrestling and agony in my soul, just at night, the subject cleared up in my mind. The Spirit led me to believe that all would come out right, and that God had yet a work for me to do; that I might be at rest; that the Lord would go forward with His work and give me strength to take any part in it that He desired. But I had not the least idea what the course of His providence would be.

On arriving at New York I found, as I have said, the mob excitement on the subject of slavery very intense. I remained but a day or two in New York, and went into the country, to the place where my family were spending the summer. On my return to New York in the fall, Mr. Leavitt came to me and said, "Brother Finney, I have ruined the *Evangelist*. I have not been as prudent as you cautioned me to be, and I have gone so far ahead of public intelligence and feeling on the subject that my subscription list is rapidly falling; and we shall not be able to continue its publication beyond the first of January unless you can do something to bring the paper back to public favor again." [Finney had helped to form the paper in the beginning.]

I told him my health was such that I did not know what I could do; but I would make it a subject of prayer. He said if I could write a series of articles on revivals, he had no doubt it would restore the paper immediately to public favor. After considering it a day or two, I proposed to preach a course of lectures to my people, on revivals of religion, which he might report for his paper. He caught at this at once. Says he, "That is the very thing"; and in the next number of his paper he advertised the course of lectures.

This had the effect he desired, and he soon after told me that the subscription list was very rapidly increasing; and, stretching out his long arms, he said, "I have as many new subscribers every day as would fill my arms with papers, to supply them each with a single number." He had told me before, that his subscription list had fallen off at the rate of sixty a day. But now he said it was increasing more rapidly than it ever had decreased.

I began the course of lectures immediately, and continued them through the winter, preaching one each week. Mr. Leavitt could not write shorthand, but would sit and take notes, abridging what he wrote in such a way that he could understand it himself; and then the next day he would sit down and fill out his notes and send them to the press. I did not see what he had reported until I saw it published in his paper.

I did not myself write the lectures, of course; they are wholly extemporaneous. I did not make up my mind, from time to time, what the next lecture should be until I saw his report of my last. Then I could see what was the next question that would naturally need discussion.

Brother Leavitt's reports were meager, as it respects the

matter contained in the lectures. The lectures averaged, if I remember right, not less than an hour and three quarters in their delivery. But all that he could catch and report could be read, probably, in thirty minutes.

These lectures were afterward published in a book and called *Finney's Lectures on Revivals.* Twelve thousand copies of them were sold, as fast as they could be printed. And here, for the glory of Christ, I would say, that they have been reprinted in England and France; they were translated into Welsh; and on the continent were translated into French and, I believe, into German; and were very extensively circulated throughout Europe and the colonies of Great Britain. They were, I presume, to be found wherever the English language is spoken.

After they had been printed in Welsh, the Congregational ministers of the Principality of Wales, at one of their public meetings, appointed a committee to inform me of the great revival that had resulted from the translation of those lectures into the Welsh language. This they did by letter.

One publisher in London informed me that his father had published eighty thousand volumes of them. These revival lectures, meager as was the report of them, and feeble as they were in themselves, have been instrumental, as I have learned, in promoting revivals in England, and Scotland, and Wales, on the continent in various places, in Canada East and West, in Nova Scotia, and in some of the islands of the sea.

But this was not man's wisdom. Let the reader remember that long day of agony and prayer at sea, that God would do something to forward the work of revivals and enable me, if he desired to do it, to take such a course as to help forward the work. I felt certain then that my prayers would be answered; and I have regarded all that I have since been able to accomplish, as, in a very important sense, an answer to the prayers of that day.

The spirit of prayer came upon me as a sovereign grace, bestowed upon me without the least merit, and despite all my sinfulness. He pressed my soul in prayer until I was enabled to prevail; and through infinite riches of grace in Christ Jesus, I have been many years witnessing the wonderful results of that day of wrestling with God. In answer to that day's agony, He has continued to give me the spirit of prayer.*

Charles G. Finney, an Autobiography, pp. 324, 328-331.

BIBLIOGRAPHY

Charles G. Finney, an Autobiography, Old Tappan, Fleming H. Revell, n.d. Copyright: The Trustees of Oberlin College 1876; Copyright renewed 1908.

Revivals of Religion, Old Tappan, Fleming H. Revell, n.d. (*Finney's Lectures on Revivals*)

Reflections on Revival, compiled by Donald Dayton, Minneapolis, Bethany Fellowship, Inc., 1979 (*Letters on Revivals*)